T0011426

ANIMAL MYTHS

EXPLODED BY SCIENCE

by Robin Twiddy

BEARPORT
PUBLISHING

Minneapolis, Minnesota

Credits

All images are courtesy of Shutterstock.com, unless otherwise specified. With thanks to Getty Images, Thinkstock Photo, and iStockphoto. Front Cover – Tomacco, Crystal Eye Studio, Cactus Studio, Top Vector Studio. 4–5 – DC Studio, AnonymousUnknown author, Public domain, via Wikimedia Commons. 6–7 – 2p2play, begun1983, Dmitry Galaganov, Igor Shoshin, Nature's Charm, LEAP STUDIOS. 8–9 – Igor Shoshin, Raggedstone, Tonhom1009, zhukovvvlad. 10–11 – Karel Bartik, LegART, Trygve Finkelsen, Marmaduke Arundel "Duke" Wetherell, Public domain, via Wikimedia Commons. 12–13 – Anne Webber, Good luck images, Oleksandr Lytvynenko, Pattarapong Kumlert, Vladimir Konstantinov. 14–15 – Beautiful landscape, Martin Pelanek, Natali Samoro, Peter Krejzl, Valentina Razumova. 16–17 – HANA, Katrina Brown, Richard Peterson, Rob Bayer, S. Aratrak. 18–19 – Paolo Trovo, Trond_Berntsen, LeCire, Public domain, via Wikimedia Commons, Jeff Carter / HowStuffWorks, CC BY 2.5 https://creativecommons.org/licenses/by/2.5>, via Wikimedia Commons. 20–21 – Chinch, Chompoo Suriyo, D. Kucharski K. Kucharska, lukeruk, Matt Knoth. 22–23 – Nick Greaves, PRESSLAB, Y-Rex, CC BY-SA 4.0 https://creativecommons.org/licenses/by-sa/4.0>, via Wikimedia Commons. 24–25 – https://creativecommons.org/licenses/by-sa/4.0>, via Wikimedia Commons, dejsak mano, KieferPix, RTimages. 26–27 – Elena11, Fotokon, Raggedstone. 28–29 – Beth Ruggiero-York, Brian Lasenby, Rudmer Zwerver, sirtravelalot. 30–31 – Art_Photo, ProStockStudio.

Bearport Publishing Company Product Development Team

President: Jen Jenson; Director of Product Development: Spencer Brinker; Managing Editor: Allison Juda; Associate Editor: Naomi Reich; Associate Editor: Tiana Tran; Senior Designer: Colin O'Dea; Associate Designer: Elena Klinkner; Associate Designer: Kayla Eggert; Product Development Specialist: Anita Stasson

CONTENTS

Welcome to TNT

TOTALLY NOT TRUE

The world is full of mysteries. Strange things happen every day. We might have trouble explaining some of them. That's where science comes in!

UFO?

Scientists **investigate** things to try and understand them. They do this using something called the scientific method.

SCIENCE

Light the science TNT and run!

TNT uses the scientific method to blow up totally not true things. *Bang!* Over the following pages, we will gather **evidence** for the unexplained. Then, we'll test that evidence against scientific facts. Let's find out what gets blown up by science!

The Scientific Method

The scientific method uses these steps.

STEP 1:
Ask a question.

Is a Bigfoot eating out of my garbage cans?

STEP 2:
Make a guess.

Yes. The cans keep getting knocked over.

STEP 3:
Find evidence.

Set up a camera to record the cans.

STEP 4:
Answer your question.

Nope. It's something about the size of a fox!

STEP 5:
Ask a new question, and do it again.

This time, I wonder if a fox is eating out of my garbage cans.

Warning! Some evidence in this book may be misleading or have a different explanation. Look out for this stamp.

MISLEADING
WARNING
EVIDENCE

ARE YOU READY TO
BLOW UP SOME MYTHS
WITH SCIENCE?

Bigfoot

What is Bigfoot?

Bigfoot is said to be a large, humanlike ape that lives in the forests of North America. People who believe Bigfoot is real point to certain evidence.

Hundreds of possible Bigfoot prints have been found since 1958.

Giant Footprints

In 1958, a set of giant, humanlike footprints were found in the woods.

Video Footage

The first video recording of Bigfoot is from 1967. This fuzzy footage shows a tall, hairy figure walking through the woods on two legs.

Since then, things that look like Bigfoot have been captured on film many times.

Samples

Hair and **stool** samples have been found near some Bigfoot sightings.

Bigfoot Calls

Many people say they've heard strange sounds in places where Bigfoot has been sighted. Some of these Bigfoot calls have been recorded.

A RECORDING DEVICE

BAD SCIENCE, GET READY TO BE BLOWN UP!

Video Evidence

Since the first footage, video technology has gotten better and easier to use. We should have seen clearer videos by now. But after 50 years, that first video of Bigfoot is still considered the best footage. Many experts think this is because it's easier to fake a sighting on old, fuzzy film than with a new digital camera.

We still don't have any videos longer than a few seconds.

Hair and Stool Samples

Scientists and the FBI have tested hair and stool samples thought to be from Bigfoot. Tests show the samples came from common animals, such as deer, bears, wolves, and even humans.

Bigfoot Calls

Experts in animal calls say the sounds reported as Bigfoot noises are too different to all be from the same kind of animal. There is no way of knowing which animals made these noises by the sounds alone.

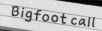

Bigfoot call

A

60

It has also been revealed that the first set of "Bigfoot" footprints were a trick!

EXPLODED BY SCIENCE!

The Loch Ness Monster

What Is the Loch Ness Monster?

Loch Ness is a deep lake in the Scottish Highlands. People have claimed to see a large creature in the water.

The Photograph

In 1934, a photograph appeared in a newspaper. It showed a long-necked creature in Loch Ness.

The Loch Ness Monster?

Loch Ness Monster's Footprint Found!

In 1933, a newspaper sent hunter Marmaduke Wetherell to find the creature. He found large footprints and guessed they belonged to an animal about 20 feet (6 m) long.

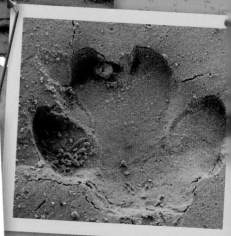

SKELETON OF A PLESIOSAUR

Could It Be a Plesiosaur?

Plesiosaurs were ocean reptiles that lived at the same time as dinosaurs. **Eyewitness** reports describe a creature with the same features as this animal. The photo from the paper looks similar, too. Could the monster be a plesiosaur?

Sonar Search

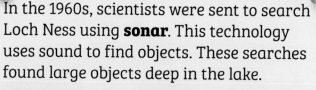
In the 1960s, scientists were sent to search Loch Ness using **sonar**. This technology uses sound to find objects. These searches found large objects deep in the lake.

Sonar readings

COUNTDOWN TO DESTRUCTION

Fake Footprint!

Scientists made plaster **casts** of the footprints found by Wetherell. They discovered the prints were all exactly the same—and were the shape of a hippo foot. Some think Wetherell made them using a stuffed hippo foot.

They match!

A HIPPO FOOT

Fake Photo!

In 1994, it was revealed that the first photo of the Loch Ness monster was a trick. The picture was of a doll head attached to a toy submarine.

Toy submarine

SCIENC

Not a Plesiosaur!

Scientists tested the water in Loch Ness for plesiosaur **DNA**. They found none. Also, there wouldn't have been enough room in the lake for such large creatures to survive.

All living things have DNA. Scientists can look at DNA to see what kind of creature it's from.

EXPLODED BY SCIENCE!

AN EEL

Suspicious Sonar

Scientists think the sonar readings of large objects were probably showing big eels or groups of fish.

Animal Behavior

We may have heard many things about animal behavior, but are they even true?

Fish Thoughts

You may have heard that goldfish have terrible memories. Or that they can only remember things for three seconds.

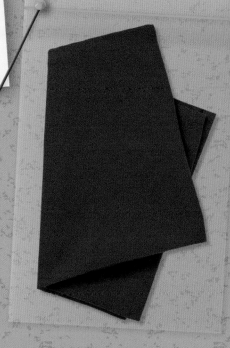

Red Rage

People say the color red makes bulls angry. When **matadors** shake red cloths, it causes bulls to charge.

14

Lemming Leap

Lemmings throw themselves off cliffs when their numbers get too large.

Wormy Ways

When an earthworm is cut in half, each end grows into a new worm.

Stinky Shapes

Wombat poop is cube shaped.

BYE BYE, BAD SCIENCE!

DEPA
DEBU

Memory Madness

Goldfish can remember things from weeks, months, and even years ago!

Lots of scientific investigations and experiments show that goldfish have good memories.

EVEN A WHITE FLAG WOULD GET A BULL TO CHARGE.

False Flag

Bulls are color-blind. They can't even see red! The color isn't what's grabbing their attention—it's the movement of the cloth.

EXPLODED BY SCIENCE!

Movie Myth

In 1958, filmmakers wanted exciting footage of lemming behavior for their movie. So, they pushed a group of the animals off a cliff. This convinced many people of the myth we know today.

PROD.

DIRECTOR

SLATE

DATE

We've been led on!

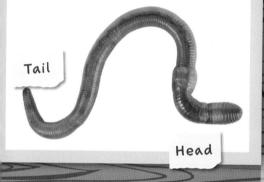

Tail

Head

Half an Earthworm Is Just Half an Earthworm

The half of an earthworm with a head may live on and grow a new tail. But the tail end will die.

Cubes of Truth

Wombats can indeed poop cubes! Scientists have studied how they do this. Wombats have special muscles that shape their poop into cubes.

FACT

A square poop out of a round hole?

El Chupacabra

The legend of El Chupacabra first appeared in 1995. Someone spotted a mysterious creature. Soon after, several goats were found drained of their blood. This is where the name chupacabra, or goat-sucker, came from!

Goats Sucked Dry

Goats and chickens have been found drained of blood. Other than two or three holes on the animals' necks, there was no sign of a struggle.

A GOAT KILLER?

Eyewitnesses

Hundreds of eyewitnesses have reported seeing a chupacabra. The first report described a creature that walked on two legs. It had gray skin, red eyes, and sharp fangs.

Body of Evidence

Several strange animal bodies have been found in Texas. These have been reported as possible bodies of chupacabras.

SCIENCE, DO YOUR STUFF!!!

El Chupacabra

When studied closely, the supposed victims of this creature were actually found to be full of blood! The animals only looked drained because their blood pooled in the body parts close to the ground after they died.

The goats had blood after all!

SCIENCE

Movie Mix-Up

The first description of El Chupacabra was very similar to an alien from a movie that had just come out. The eyewitness that gave the report later remembered seeing the movie days before.

Scientists have proven that eyewitnesses often blend memories and mix up details.

CINEMA TICKET
THEATER 18 / SEAT 28
ADMIT O

EMA KET
SEAT 29

POP CORN

sf mov
mar

Not a Vampire!

The creatures that were reported to be chupacabras didn't have the body parts to drink blood. They lacked the fangs of other blood-sucking creatures, such as vampire bats.

A VAMPIRE BAT

The Truth Is in the DNA

When the body of a chupacabra was tested by scientists, they discovered what it really was—a coyote with **mange**.

A coyote

EXPLODED BY SCIENCE!

The Beast of Bodmin Moor

Since 1978, police in Bodmin, England, have been baffled by reports of a large, catlike creature roaming the local **moors**. But there aren't any big cats native to England.

Cat's Eye-Witness

There have been more than a thousand sightings. Some reports are from **credible** witnesses, such as a car full of police and a reporter in the middle of a radio **broadcast**.

Dear Police,
I saw the
beast...it
was big.

MISLEADING
WARNING
EVIDENCE

Picture Evidence

The strongest pieces of evidence yet are the photos of what appear to be big cats in the Bodmin area.

A Skull Is Found!

The skull of a big cat was found where the creature was believed to live.

Government Investigation

There was so much evidence for a big cat on the moors, the government sent investigators to take a look.

READY, SET... BLOW UP!!!

Problems with Eyewitnesses

Eyewitness reports can't always be trusted. Our brains often fill in details that aren't there when we see something odd or confusing.

Eyewitness reports aren't strong enough evidence on their own!

Photographic evidence

Today, smartphones have much better cameras than they did 10 years ago. Yet, no one has a good photo or video of the beast. Without better photos today, many experts think the first were faked.

Fuzzy image

No videos

Easily faked

SCIENCE

Skull

Experts found bits of cockroaches native to the tropics in the skull. They also found knife marks showing the skin of the animal had been removed by a person. The experts think the skull was brought to England as part of a leopard-skin rug.

IT'S FROM A RUG!

The Government

The government found no evidence of big cats on the moors. However, they aren't ready to rule it out. They just need more evidence!

Y NEWS

e - Lifestyle - Travel - Sport - Weather

Government Can't Find Beast

Here, kitty kitty! Britain's big cat enthusiasts are disappointed once again at the findings, or lack thereof, of the government's Bodmin investigation team. Despite dozens of man-hours invested in hunting the famed feline fiend, no significant findings have been une
Here, kitty kitty! B
are disapp
on

Here, kitty kitty! Britain's big cat enthusiasts are disappointed once again at the findings, or lack thereof, of the government's Bodmin investigation team. Despite dozens of man-hours invested in hunting the famed feline fiend, no significant findings have been unearthed.
Here, kitty kitty! Britain's big
are disappointed on
or lack the
in

MORE EVIDENCE NEEDED

The Mothman

MISLEADING
WARNING
EVIDENCE

Independent Eyewitnesses

In 1966, the small town of Point Pleasant, West Virginia, was **terrorized** by what looked like a large, birdlike man with red eyes. The strange creature soon became known as the Mothman.

Eyewitness

On November 12, five men saw a human-shaped figure flying overhead.

Both reports were given separately before news of the sightings was shared.

Eyewitness

On November 15, two couples told police their car had been chased by a dark figure with huge wings.

Mothman's Movements

The creature was described as flying almost 100 miles per hour (160 kph).

Artist drawing of the Mothman

There were eight more sightings in the few days following the original reports.

The Mothman Mutant?

Many of the early sightings happened near a place that made **ammunitions** during World War II (1939–1945). Some locals believed secret experiments might also have been happening there.

Could the Mothman have been the result of a dangerous experiment?

Unusually Large Feathers

Some very large feathers have been found around Point Pleasant. Could these have been from the Mothman?

DEPA
DEB

Independent Eyewitnesses

Eyewitnesses from the first sightings reported seeing something with white wings that was about 7 ft (2 m) tall. Unusual, yes. However, we shouldn't jump to conclusions.

SCIEN

When using the scientific method, we need to look for a pattern before making a decision. We need more than two sightings to have a pattern.

The world's heaviest flying bird is the great bustard. It weighs about 30 pounds (14 kg). Scientists believe feathered flight for a much heavier creature is impossible.

Although people claim to have seen giant feathers, no evidence of a large feather has been presented.

SANDHILL CRANES

There is a simpler explanation than a mutant experiment. The sandhill crane is a large bird that is almost as tall as an adult human. It has a 7-ft (2-m) wingspan and a huge red spot around its eyes. Even though sandhill cranes don't live in Point Pleasant, they are known to pass through the area as they **migrate**.

The description of this bird fits with many of the eyewitness statements.

EXPLODED BY
SCIENCE!

Science Saves the Day

Working Scientifically

Even though it's fun to think about mysterious creatures such as Bigfoot or the Loch Ness monster, you should take a closer look using the scientific method. That means gathering evidence and information, asking questions, and coming up with a fact-based guess.

Testing for Truth

Then, put your guess to the test! You can do this by conducting experiments to see if your guess is right. And most of all, you should keep blowing up myths with your TNT of science!

When you are unsure what is true and what is not, remember that science can help!

GLOSSARY

ammunitions objects fired from a weapon

broadcast a show that is played on television or radio

casts hard shells molded into shapes

credible believable and trustworthy

DNA material present in all living things that carries information about how a thing will look and act

evidence objects or information that can be used to prove whether something is true

eyewitness someone who has seen something and can describe it

investigate to search for information about something

mange a skin disease causing itchy rashes and loss of hair or fur

matadors people who fight bulls

migrate to move from one place to another at a certain time of year

moors areas of land that are open and wet

sonar technology that uses sound to locate objects underwater

stool poop

terrorized made very afraid

INDEX

READ MORE

Finan, Catherine C. *Animals (X–treme Facts: Science).* Minneapolis: Bearport Publishing Company, 2021.

Hyde, Natalie. *Animal Oddballs (Astonishing Animals).* New York: Crabtree Publishing Company, 2020.

Thompson, Kim. *True Facts on Animals (Can You Believe It's True?).* New York: Crabtree Publishing, 2023.

LEARN MORE ONLINE

1. Go to **www.factsurfer.com** or scan the QR code below.
2. Enter "**Not True Animals**" into the search box.
3. Click on the cover of this book to see a list of websites.